Dominik Heinz

Opportunities and Risks of Social Media Tools for the Economy

GRIN Publishing

Bibliographic information published by the German National Library:

The German National Library lists this publication in the National Bibliography;
detailed bibliographic data are available on the Internet at http://dnb.dnb.de .

Imprint:

Copyright © 2009 GRIN Verlag, Open Publishing GmbH
Print and binding: Books on Demand GmbH, Norderstedt Germany
ISBN: 978-3-656-14905-7

GRIN - Your knowledge has value

Since its foundation in 1998, GRIN has specialized in publishing academic texts by students, college teachers and other academics as e-book and printed book. The website www.grin.com is an ideal platform for presenting term papers, final papers, scientific essays, dissertations and specialist books.

Visit us on the internet:

http://www.grin.com/

http://www.facebook.com/grincom

http://www.twitter.com/grin_com

Assignment

Opportunities and Risks of Social Media Tools
For the Economy

Master of Business Administration (MBA)

Module: Economics

Author: Dominik Heinz

Stuttgart, December 19th 2009

I.   Content

II.   Introduction

The globalization has been strongly leveraged by the internet and the new internet technologies. Using new internet technologies, people and companies are communicating and col-
laborating more than ever. Information flow and information flow control are emerging tasks
of people, companies, governments and other social groups. Social web tools are of key interest when talking of information flow and the attempt of some sort of control. Menace of
chance - is the economy suffering or profiteering from the fast growing internet communication traffic? This paper will try to spot on the most important aspects and how they could impact local and global economies.

III.   Executive Summary

This assignment elaborates the opportunities and risks of social media tools for the economy.
The first paragraphs will show what social media tools are and how they work. The second
paragraph will provide an overview of the topic swarm intelligence. The conjunction of the
social media tools with their ability to support the swarm intelligence effect will lead to the
conclusion of this assignment: Social media tools can generate swarm intelligence effects
which can greatly support the economy. As a disadvantage, social media tools support uncon-
trolled distribution of private information and intellectual property which might hold many
dangers for the economy.

IV.   Abbreviations

1 T&D – Training and Development
2 R&D – Research and Development
3 IP – Intellectual Property

1   Definitions

1.1   Applied Terminology

- Social Media: collective content created by any individual of that collective;
- Social Media tools: tools that help individuals collaborate, communicate, and access their collective content;
- Swarm: a swarm is a population of individuals that tend to cluster together although any individual is independent and shows a random behavior;
- Crowd: a crowd is a large group of individuals;

1.2   Economy

The paradigm for economies existence is the scarcity of goods. Gregory Mankiw phrased the economy to be the study of how society manages its scarce resources.[1] Every individual within a society is struggling for getting most out of these scarce resources. Thus, for economics science, the distribution behavior of these individuals is of key interest.

2   Social Media

2.1   Definition

The term "Social Media Tools" describes websites and tools that rely on people, who are using them in an interactive manner. The content is not being provided by a super user, but by the normal users themselves. Everybody using a social media tool is part of the creation process. The usage change of internet based tools and websites from a read-only way to this interactive style has been labeled as the change from "Web 1.0" to "Web 2.0". However, the term "Web 2.0" has never been completely accepted within business circles. As a matter of fact, the usage of the term is decreasing.[2]

Today the term "Social Media Tools" is used. L. Lafko and D. Brake define three basic rules concerning social media:

1. Social Media is all about enabling conversations;
2. You cannot control conversations, but you can influence them;
3. Influence is the bedrock upon which all economically viable relationships are built;[3]

2.2   History

Toward the year 2000, internet businesses and offerings grew overwhelmingly fast. Unfortunately, as it soon turned out the enormous growth was not much more than a speculative bubble. The internet business collapsed dramatically in the year 2001. It was at that point when key players of the internet business like Tim O'Reilly and the company MediaLive International began to wonder whether the "dot-com collapse marked some kind of turning point for the web, such that a call to action like "Web 2.0" might make sense".[4] Since this turning point, all online tools, which are used in an interactive, user-driven way, were labeled as "Web 2.0" applications. A large amount of consulting and internet companies worked hard to advertise the term "Web 2.0", yet failed most likely because the term "Web 2.0" was too artificial. Today, the term "Social Media Tools" is increasingly accepted as it simply describes the tool's purpose better than the theoretical "Web 2.0" term.

2.3   The Term Social Web

Social webs are composed by individuals who are connected to each other. The connection can be used for different purposes such as personal and professional networking, information exchange, and updates. A social web should provide the following information about people:

- **Identity**: who are you? Depending on the purpose of the social web, different personal or professional aspects are of informative need.

- **Reputation**: what do people think you stand for? Within a social web, a user needs to create a personal or professional profile. Users try to create a preferred image of them that may differ from reality. The proper term for this phenomenon is "reputation management".

- **Presence**: where are you? Technologies geared toward the increase of a user's presence are currently growing on the internet market. A popular tool is called "Twitter" and is used for small status messages.

- **Relationships**: who are you connected with? Who do you trust? Connections between users describe personal or professional relationships. Most tools have the disadvantage in that they do not show the quality of the relationship.

- **Conversations**: what do you discuss with others? Conversations in social webs are performed in the same way as in direct inter-personal exchange. Forums and emails are the most important, and well-known media.

2.4   The Term Wiki

A wiki (the Hawaiian word for 'quick'), is a collaborative web site that allows virtually everybody to edit its pages. Usually, a website is created by a single person, team or company. Subsequently, the website's content is accessible to internet users around the globe. A wiki website is not created by a single person, team or company. Its base construct is created and published to the internet. As a consequence, every user has the possibility and the right to create, change or delete articles, pictures, and movies within a wiki page. Bo Leuf and Ward Cunningham have published a book called "The Wiki Way - Quick Collaboration on the Web." This title describes the phenomenon in a nutshell: Wikis are about collaboration. Users are working together on a central knowledge base, a base constituted by the user's collective knowledge, ergo the steep increase of contemporary discussion concerning the term "collective intelligence".[5]

3   Collective Intelligence

3.1   Foundation

In James Surowiecki's seminal book *Swarm Intelligence – Why the Many are Smarter than the Few*, he explores a deceptively simple idea with profound implications: large groups of people are smarter than an elite few, no matter how brilliant this smaller group is, that is in their heightened ability to solving problems, fostering innovation, and making correct decisions.[6] In the context of wiki and the usage of social web tools, the increasing collaborative behavior of individuals is leading to a construct comparable to Surowiecki's notion of a collective intelligence.

3.2   Swarm Intelligence

Bees or Ants are most commonly described when talking from swarm intelligence. These small insects are normally living in a large population. Every individual seems to move independent in a random way, but actually the collective works together in a very effective way. Russel C. Eberhard, Professor at the IUPUI concludes that behavior to be manifested within the social behavior of the insect individuals. He states three key phrases:

- Social behavior increases the ability of an individual to adapt;
- There is a relationship between adaptability and intelligence;
- Intelligence arises from interactions among individuals;[7]

3.3   Assumption

Eberhard states intelligence arises from interactions among individuals. If Surowiecki's thesis that a crowd of individuals is always smarter than single persons is correct, then society should try to raise interactions among individuals.

4   Economic Opportunities of Social Media Tools

4.1   Challenges of common paradigms

Prof H. Sauermann states in his class about economics and the FOM Graduate School of Business that "the economy overall is weigh to complex to understand". The author of this paper would like to extend this statement and add "for a single person". Economics is a too complex topic for a single person to understand. The most pressing question of this paper is though who else could understand economic issues.

4.2   Crowdsourcing for Complex Problem Solving

4.2.1   Definition Crowdsourcing

Trending topic in the economists world of the last years was a phenomenon called „outsourcing". When a firm's management makes the decision to give specific task that traditionally had been accomplished by specific party of the firm, to an external vendor or contractor, it *sources that task out*. Another approach is not to source the task out to a vendor or contractor, but to an unlimited large group of people called "the crowd". As a result the term "crowdsourcing" is emerging. Jeff Howe elaborates the topic crowdsourcing in his book *Why the Power of the Crowd Is Driving the Future of Business*[8] using the example of open source software development.

4.2.2   Definition Crowd

An accepted definition of crowd is that of a large group of individuals in the same physical environment, sharing a common goal (e.g. people going to a rock concert or a football match). The individuals in a crowd may act in a different way than when they are alone or in a small group.[9] Furthermore an individual of a crowd is typically not a specialist in solving the crowd's common goal. As the problem solving capability of a crowd increases with the number of their individuals, quantity is more important as quality. The Wired magazine lists the five principles of the new labor pool:

1. The crowd is **dispersed** – geographically and in matters of skill, available time, and personal attributes;

2. The crowd has **short attention span** – jobs needs to be cut to micro-chunks;

3. The crowd is full of specialists; (In the authors opinion this principle is not correct neither important. The size of the crowd produces crowd effects and not the abilities of their individuals.)

4. The crowd **produces mostly crap** – any open call for submissions will elicit mostly junk;

5. The crowd **finds the best stuff**; [10]

If these requirements have to be translated into technical requirements, a crowdsourcing tool has to be easy to use and very scalable.

4.2.3 Examples using Crowdsourcing using Social Media Tools

The Wired magazine described in an article called *The Rise of Crowdsourcing* five examples of common crowdsourcing projects and how they impact the market. In the following list two interesting projects will be described shortly:

1. A website called *iStockPhoto*[11] where anyone can upload and sell self-made pictures. As camera equipment got cheaper and better the last years, amateur pictures reach a professional quality standard. A having a crowd of photographers, agencies are able to get better and cheaper pictures compared to the professional suppliers.

2. *InnoCentive*[12] is the name of a project, where a crowd is used to solve scientific challenges. The project tries to unite a web community of scientists, engineers, professionals and entrepreneurs worldwide who collaborate. [12] The overall goal is to crowdsource corporate R&D tasks to lower cost.

5   Economic Risks of Social Media Tools

5.1   Patents and Intellectual Property

5.1.1   Definition

Very broadly, intellectual property (IP) means the legal rights which result from intellectual activity in the industrial, scientific, literary and artistic fields.[13] These legal rights are granted by a government to individuals like persons or companies. The term intellectual property most commonly describes intangible products. These have greater significance for economists than they do for lawyers.[14] Tangible protected intellectual property is described as being a patent.

5.1.2   IP Sharing

Beneath collaboration and communication, IP sharing is one of the most important features of a social media tool. IP is created by individuals and crowds. IP is being transferred from one individual to another. IP is created by an individual and then changed by another. IP is created by a crowd and deleted by an individual.

This principal is fundamentally colliding with governmental IP protection. Critics of intellectual property regulations content that restrictions could be tantamount to violating free speech and information rights.[15]

Actually there is no solution to this ongoing discussion. In the authors opinion the reason for this dilemma is manifested on the fundamental difference between the individual focused 'homo universalis' (the universally capable individual) paradigm and the crowd focused 'vox populi' (the voice of the crowd) paradigm. The current only possible solution is a productive coexistence.

5.1.3   Fast News Distribution

Social media tools leverage news distribution. If a firm leaks information, these are getting distributed using social media tools weigh faster than in the past. If an individual gets to know the private information or IP, the crowd and thus anyone knows. An economical risk of social media tools is the fast distribution of private information and IP.

5.2   Control on Information and Conversation History

The German newspaper FAZ released an article called *On the quest for a rubber* released 2009.[16] The article talks about the fact, that the internet does never forget about things and how this could harm individual's reputation. It is correct, that internet tools normally do not have a data aging mechanism which deletes outdates entries, pictures and other data.

This circumstance could harm individual's reputation as individuals tend to forget about old entries, statements or pictures or underlay the misleading assumption, that data entered on websites is private. But this is the personal risk of the data sharing individual. The crowd and thus the economy does not suffer from the broken reputation of individuals.

6 Summary

As this paper has shown, social media tools can solve an immense amount of challenges within the economics area. Used in a cross cultural understandable context and framework, these tools increase the knowledge exchange, promote interactions of companies and improve networking options. In this way they productively enhance the quality and quantity among individuals contributing to the success of themselves and the society. However, one has to be aware of the disadvantages within the many advantages to avoid mistakes and a harmful usage of these tools. Used properly and professionally for networking and knowledge management, social web tools entail yet another key to the success of the future and development of a society. Social web tools will boost mankind's advancement because the crowd is always smarter.

7   Appendix - Sources:

1   Mankiw, Gregory
    Principles of Economics (p.4)

2   Rusak, Sergey
    http://www.progressiveadvertiser.com/web-2-0-becoming-an-outdated-term/
    Accessed: 11\19\2009

3   L. Lafko / D. Brake (2009)
    The Social Media Bible, Tactics, Tools, and Strategies for Business (p.52)

4   Tim O'Reilly (2005)
    http://oreilly.com/web2/archive/what-is-web-20.html
    Accessed: 11\19\2009

5   Bo Leuf, Ward Cunninghama (2008)
    The Wiki way - quick collaboration on the Web (p.448)

6   James Surowiecki (2004)
    The Wisdom of Crowds - Why the Many are Smarter than the Few (p.1)

7   unknown source

8   Jeff Howe (2008)
    Crowdsourcing - why the power of the crowd is driving the future of business (p.1)

9   M. E. Roloff (1981)
    Interpersonal Communication - The Social Exchange Approach (p.1)

10 Jeff Howe (2006)
    http://www.wired.com/wired/archive/14.06/labor.html
    Accessed: 12\15\2009

11 iStockPhoto
    http://www.istockphoto.com/introduction.php
    Accessed: 12\15\2009

12 InnoCentive
    http://www.innocentive.com/corporate.php
    Accessed: 12\15\2009

13 World Intellectual Property Organization (1997)
    Introduction to intellectual property: theory and practice (p.3)

14 Keith Eugene Maskus (2008)

Intellectual property, growth and trade (p.36)

15   George Brown (2008)

        Social Media 100 Success Secrets: Social Media, Web 2.0 User-Generated (p.132)

16   Nadine Oberhuber (2009)

        http://www.faz.net/s/Rub2F3F4B59BC1F4E6F8AD8A246962CEBCD/Doc~E3AA66

        55D0A514600BE4EBAB3C2BF5503~ATpl~Ecommon~Scontent.html

        Accessed: 12\08\2009